Beyond the Players

Trainers

by Allan Morey

Ideas for Parents and Teachers

Bullfrog Books let children practice reading informational text at the earliest reading levels. Repetition, familiar words, and photo labels support early readers.

Before Reading
- **Discuss the cover photo. What does it tell them?**
- **Look at the picture glossary together. Read and discuss the words.**

Read the Book
- **"Walk" through the book and look at the photos. Let the child ask questions. Point out the photo labels.**
- **Read the book to the child, or have him or her read independently.**

After Reading
- **Prompt the child to think more. Ask: Have you ever seen trainers at sporting events? How do they help athletes?**

Bullfrog Books are published by Jump!
5357 Penn Avenue South
Minneapolis, MN 55419
www.jumplibrary.com

Copyright © 2024 Jump! International copyright reserved in all countries. No part of this book may be reproduced in any form without written permission from the publisher.

Library of Congress Cataloging-in-Publication Data

Names: Morey, Allan, author.
Title: Trainers / Allan Morey.
Description: Minneapolis, MN: Jump!, Inc., [2024]
Series: Beyond the players | Includes index.
Audience: Ages 5–8
Identifiers: LCCN 2023028600 (print)
LCCN 2023028601 (ebook)
ISBN 9798889966531 (hardcover)
ISBN 9798889966548 (paperback)
ISBN 9798889966555 (ebook)
Subjects: LCSH: Athletic trainers—Juvenile literature.
Classification: LCC GV428.7 .M67 2024 (print)
LCC GV428.7 (ebook)
DDC 796.092—dc23/eng/20230725
LC record available at https://lccn.loc.gov/2023028600
LC ebook record available at https://lccn.oc.gov/2023028601

Editor: Jenna Gleisner
Designer: Emma Almgren-Bersie

Photo Credits: PeopleImages.com - Yuri A/Shutterstock, cover; pixelheadphoto digitalskillet/Shutterstock, 1; New Africa/Shutterstock, 3; Victor Velter/Shutterstock, 4; Sport In Pictures/Alamy, 5; ALAN OLIVER/Alamy, 6–7; dotshock/Shutterstock, 8–9, 23br; TSViPhoto/Shutterstock, 10; Anchiy/iStock, 10–11; TORWAISTUDIO/Shutterstock, 12–13, 23tl; SeventyFour/iStock, 14; Frank Gunn/The Canadian Press/AP Images, 15; Sebastian Gollnow/picture-alliance/dpa/AP Images, 16–17; Aaron M. Sprecher/AP Images, 18; Mike Groll/AP Images, 19; matimix/Shutterstock, 20–21, 23bl; Africa Studio/Shutterstock, 22tl; South_agency/iStock, 22tr; HRAUN/iStock, 22bl; Ralph R. Echtinaw/Shutterstock, 22br; Shunevych Serhii/Shutterstock, 23tr; Jiri Hera/Shutterstock, 24.

Printed in the United States of America at Corporate Graphics in North Mankato, Minnesota.

Table of Contents

Helping Athletes 4
Part of the Team 22
Picture Glossary 23
Index 24
To Learn More 24

Helping Athletes

We watch gymnasts.

Oh, no!
He fell.
He is hurt.

Who helps? Trainers! They are part of the team.

Athletes work hard.
They care for their bodies.
Trainers help.
Mel shows Dani how to stretch.

The big game is tomorrow.
Brent needs energy.
What should he eat?
His trainer tells him.

Em lifts weights. She gets stronger. Cam watches. He makes sure she is safe.

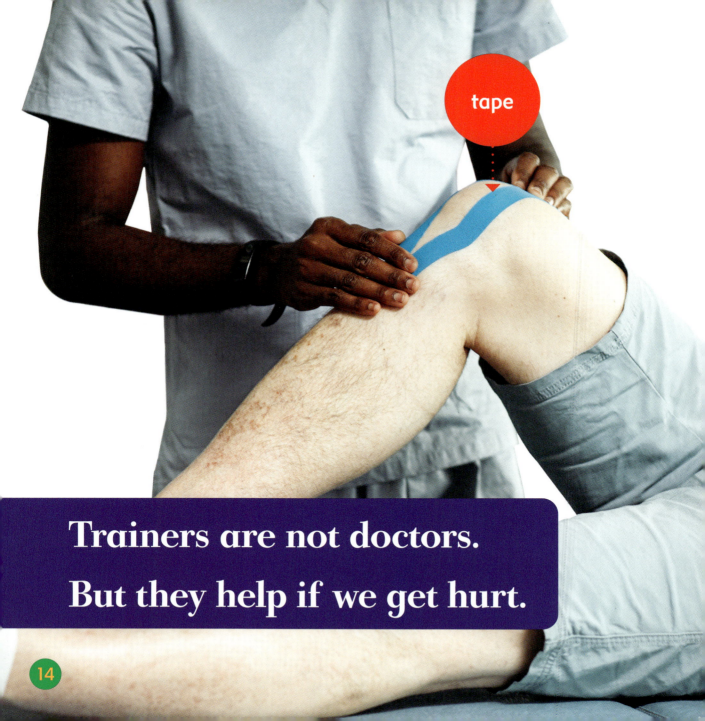

tape

Trainers are not doctors.
But they help if we get hurt.

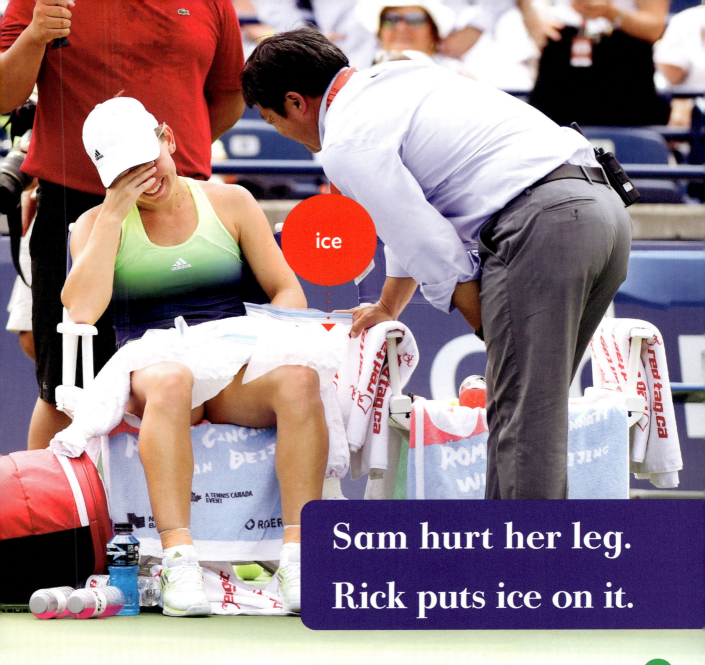

Sam hurt her leg.
Rick puts ice on it.

Players warm up.
They get ready to play.
A trainer leads
the exercises.

Trainers help during the game.

How?

They bring water.

They help after the game, too.
They check players.

Do you like fitness?

Do you want to help others?

You can be a trainer!

Part of the Team

Trainers are part of the team. How do they help athletes? Take a look!

health
Trainers talk about nutrition.

exercise
Trainers show athletes exercises.

warm up
Trainers help athletes stretch and warm up before playing.

recovery
Trainers help athletes heal and recover from injuries.

Picture Glossary

athletes
People who are trained in sports and physical exercise.

energy
The ability or strength to do things without getting tired.

fitness
How healthy and strong someone is.

stretch
To reach out your arms, legs, or body to its full length.

Index

athletes 9
bodies 9
energy 10
exercises 16
game 10, 18, 19
hurt 5, 14, 15
ice 15
safe 13
stretch 9
warm up 16
water 18
weights 13

To Learn More

Finding more information is as easy as 1, 2, 3.

❶ Go to www.factsurfer.com

❷ Enter "trainers" into the search box.

❸ Choose your book to see a list of websites.